S0-AYB-473

Jackie Robinson

by Lucia Raatma

Compass Point Early Biographies

Content Adviser: Professor Sherry L. Field,
Department of Social Science Education, College of Education,
The University of Georgia

Reading Adviser: Dr. Linda D. Labbo,
Department of Reading Education, College of Education,
The University of Georgia

SOUTH HUNTINGTON
PUBLIC LIBRARY
2 MELVILLE ROAD
HUNTINGTON STATION, N.Y. 11746

COMPASS POINT BOOKS

Minneapolis, Minnesota

*JB
Robinson
R.*

Compass Point Books
3722 West 50th Street, #115
Minneapolis, MN 55410

Visit Compass Point Books on the Internet at *www.compasspointbooks.com* or e-mail your
request to *custserv@compasspointbooks.com*

Photographs ©:

Sporting News/Archive Photos, cover; Bettmann/Corbis, cover; FPG International, 4; Archive Photos, 6, 7;
Bettmann/Corbis, 8; Sporting News/Archive Photos, 9; The Sporting News, 10; FPG International, 12; Archive Photos,
14; Sporting News/Archive Photos, 15; FPG International, 16, 18; Sporting News/Archive Photos, 19; Bettmann/Corbis,
20 top; FPG International, 20 bottom; Bettmann/Corbis, 21 top and bottom; FPG International, 22, 23; Bettmann/Corbis,
25; Reuters/Mike Segar/Archive Photos, 26; Reuters/Ray Stubblebine/Archive Photos, 27 top; Blank Archives/Archive
Photos, 27 bottom.

Editors: E. Russell Primm and Emily J. Dolbear
Photo Researcher: Svetlana Zhurkina
Photo Selector: Dawn Friedman
Design: Bradfordesign, Inc.

Library of Congress Cataloging-in-Publication Data

Raatma, Lucia.
    Jackie Robinson / by Lucia Raatma.
        p. cm. — (Compass Point early biographies)
Includes bibliographical references and index.
Summary: An introduction to the personal life and baseball career of the legendary player, Jackie
Robinson.
    ISBN 0-7565-0016-8 (hardcover : lib. bdg.)
        1. Robinson, Jackie, 1919–1972—Juvenile literature. 2. Baseball players—United States—
Biography—Juvenile literature. [1. Robinson, Jackie, 1919–1972. 2. Baseball players.
3. Afro-Americans—Biography.] I. Title. II. Series.
    GV865.R6 R32 2000
    796.357'092—dc21
                                                                            00-008667

© 2001 by Compass Point Books

All rights reserved. No part of this book may be reproduced without written permission from the publisher. The publisher takes no
responsibility for the use of any of the materials or methods described in this book, nor for the products thereof.

Printed in the United States of America.

306520008424 78

Table of Contents

A Famous Baseball Player 5

Young Athlete 6

In the Army 9

As a Baseball Player 11

Making Changes 13

Family Life 16

Making History 17

Doing His Best 18

A Baseball Success 19

After Baseball 21

Remembering Jackie Robinson 26

Important Dates in Jackie Robinson's Life 28

Glossary 29

Did You Know? 30

Want to Know More? 31

Index 32

A Famous Baseball Player

Jackie Robinson was a great baseball player. He was the first African-American to play in America's **major leagues**.

In the 1940s, there was a **color barrier** in the United States. African-Americans were not allowed to play with white players. But when Jackie Robinson entered the major leagues, all that changed.

◄ Jackie Robinson broke the color barrier playing for the Brooklyn Dodgers.

Young Athlete

Jack Roosevelt Robinson was born in Cairo, Georgia, on January 31, 1919. His family later moved and he grew up in Pasadena, California. In high school, Jackie was very good at sports.

When he was eighteen, Jackie went to a local college. He left to go to the University of California at Los Angeles in 1939. Jackie joined the football, baseball, track, and basketball teams. He became the first student to earn a **school letter** in four sports in one year. It was a great honor.

Jackie in college

◀ Young Jackie (second from left) with his family

Two years later, Jackie had to leave college. His family was having money problems and needed his help. For a time, he had a job playing football for the Los Angeles Bulldogs of California.

Jackie playing football at the University of California at Los Angeles

In the Army

In 1942, Jackie Robinson joined
the U.S. Army. At that time, the
United States was fighting in
World War II (1939–1945). Jackie
became an army officer.

Jackie in his
army uniform

Jackie faced problems in the army because
he was African-American. African-American
men were treated differently from white men
in many ways. Jackie questioned the army's
rules. The army told Jackie that he might be
put on trial for his views. He might be thrown
out of the army. He might even have to go to
jail. Finally the charges were dropped. In
1945, Jackie left the army.

9

As a Baseball Player

After he left the army, Jackie Robinson began playing baseball for the Kansas City Monarchs. This team was part of a baseball league for African-American players. This league was called the Negro League.

One day, a baseball **scout** came to watch Jackie Robinson play. The scout was from the Brooklyn Dodgers in New York. The team moved to Los Angeles later. The scout was looking for new players. He saw that Jackie was very talented. So he talked to team president Branch Rickey about Jackie Robinson.

◄ Jackie played baseball for the Kansas City Monarchs.

Making Changes

Branch Rickey felt that it was unfair to keep African-American players out of major-league baseball. He wanted African-Americans to play baseball alongside the white players.

Branch Rickey met with Jackie Robinson. He was impressed by Jackie's ability. He also knew Jackie was a brave person and a gentleman. Branch believed that he had found someone who could help change the major leagues.

On October 23, 1945, Jackie Robinson joined the Montreal Royals in Canada.

◀ Branch Rickey was the team president of the Brooklyn Dodgers.

The Montreal Royals were the Dodgers' **farm team**. (A farm team trains young talented players for its major-league team.) Jackie batted very well for the Montreal Royals that year.

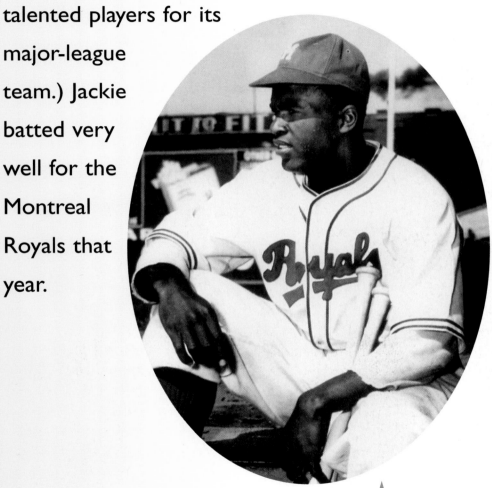

◄ Jackie Robinson signs his contract with the Montreal Royals.

Jackie in his Royals uniform

Family Life

The following year, another part of Jackie's life began. He married his longtime girlfriend, Rachel Annetta Isum. Over the years, Jackie and Rachel had three children.

Making History

In April 1947, it was time to break the color barrier. Jackie Robinson put on a Brooklyn Dodgers uniform and played his first major-league game with his white teammates.

As Jackie walked out on Ebbets Field in Brooklyn, some fans shouted at him. Even some of his own teammates made rude comments to him about his skin color. Some pitchers tried to hit him with balls when he was at bat.

On the road, there were also problems. Some hotels would not allow Jackie to stay in their rooms.

◄ Jackie and Rachel with Jackie Jr.

Doing His Best

But Jackie paid no attention to this **racism**. He had told Branch Rickey that he could stand up to these people. He knew that his job was to play the best baseball he could.

Jackie soon proved Branch Rickey right. At the end of his first season, he was named **Rookie** of the Year. That honor is given to the year's best new baseball player. And he led the National League in stolen bases.

On the road with the Dodgers

A Baseball Success

In 1949, Jackie Robinson
was the National League
batting champion. He
was also named Most
Valuable Player. Between
1949 and 1952, Jackie led
all the league's second
basemen in the number of
double plays made.

Making a catch

   He was a great hitter and a good fielder.
He also ran bases very well. Former Dodgers
manager Leo Durocher once said about Jackie,

"He didn't just come to play; he came to beat you."

Jackie was named to six all-star teams. While he was with the Dodgers, they won six National League championships. In 1955, they even won the World Series.

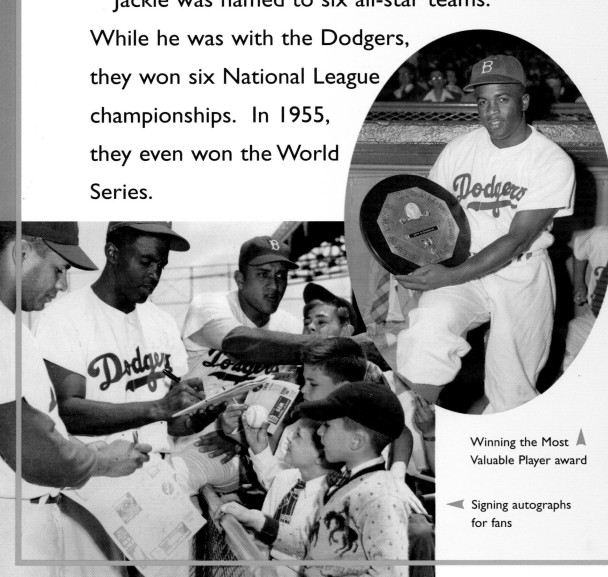

Winning the Most ⏶ Valuable Player award

◀ Signing autographs for fans

After Baseball

Jackie Robinson left baseball
the next year. The Dodgers
honored him by retiring his
number—42. Then in 1962,
Jackie Robinson was named to
the Baseball Hall of Fame. He

Jackie packs away
the number 42.

was the first African-American man to receive

that honor. Jackie
Robinson worked for
civil rights after he
stopped playing base-
ball. He knew that
racial issues were

Robinson with his
Hall of Fame plaque

21

important in the United States. He tried to
bring people of all races together.

Jackie also worked hard to help children in
communities around the country. He often
went to baseball camps to coach.

Jackie coaches at the YMCA in Harlem, New York.

◀ Jackie Robinson often spoke
out for civil rights.

On October 24, 1972, Jackie Robinson died at his home in Stamford, Connecticut. He had suffered from **diabetes** and heart problems. More than 2,500 people came to his funeral in New York City. Reverend Jesse Jackson spoke at the service.

Thousands of fans came to Jackie Robinson's funeral. ➤

Remembering Jackie Robinson

The next year, Rachel Robinson began a program in her husband's name. The program helps African-Americans and others who need money for school.

In 1982, the U.S. Postal Service printed a stamp honoring Jackie Robinson. In 1997, he received another honor. All the major-league baseball teams celebrated the fiftieth anniversary of Jackie's first game in the major

Rachel Robinson at the Jackie Robinson Foundation annual dinner

leagues. People celebrated his life for a whole season. Jackie Robinson's impact, or effect, on baseball and on his country will last forever.

The words on Jackie Robinson's grave speak of his influence. They read: "A life is not important except for the impact it has on other lives."

President Bill Clinton, Rachel Robinson, and baseball commissioner Bud Selig celebrating the fiftieth anniversary of Jackie's first major-league game

A postage stamp honoring Jackie

Important Dates in Jackie Robinson's Life

1919	Born on January 31 in Cairo, Georgia
1939	Enters the University of California at Los Angeles
1941	Leaves college
1942	Joins the U.S. Army
1945	Leaves the army
1945	Joins the Montreal Royals
1946	Marries Rachel Annetta Isum
1947	Plays his first major-league game; is named Rookie of the Year
1949	Is the league's batting champion; is named Most Valuable Player
1956	Retires from baseball
1962	Is named to the Baseball Hall of Fame
1972	Dies on October 24 in Stamford, Connecticut

Glossary

civil rights—the rights and freedoms of a citizen

color barrier—the separation of the races that kept African-Americans from playing baseball with whites

diabetes—a disease in which there is too much sugar in a person's blood

double play—a play in baseball in which two players are put out

farm team—a team that trains young talented players for a major-league team

major leagues—the league in which the best baseball teams in America play

racism—a belief that any race is better than another

rookie—a new player

school letter—the initial of a school awarded for skill in sports

scout—a person who looks for new, talented players

Did You Know?

- Jackie Robinson was kicked out of a game in 1948 for arguing with an umpire. Jackie was very pleased, however, because he had been treated like any other baseball player.

- In 1950, Jackie Robinson starred as himself in the film *The Jackie Robinson Story*.

- Jackie Robinson once said, "Above anything else, I hate to lose."

- Jackie Robinson wrote his life story. It's called *I Never Had It Made*.

Want to Know More?

At the Library

Cooper, Elisha. *Ballpark*. New York: Greenwillow, 1998.

Dingle, Derek T. *First in the Field: Baseball Hero Jackie Robinson*. New York: Disney Press, 1998.

Golenbock, Peter. *Teammates*. New York: Harcourt Brace, 1990.

On the Web

The Jackie Robinson Interview
http://www.inthegardenstate.com/unionmedia/robinson/Intro.htm
For a timeline of Jackie Robinson's life and a 1962 interview

The Jackie Robinson Society
http://www.utexas.edu/students/jackie/index.html
For articles about the baseball player, quotes by and about Robinson, and photographs

Through the Mail

The Jackie Robinson Society
1712 Woodward, #104
Austin, TX 73301
For Jackie Robinson's statistics

On the Road

National Baseball Hall of Fame and Museum
25 Main Street
P.O. Box 590
Cooperstown, NY 13326
888/425-5633
To see exhibits about the greatest baseball players of all time

Index

African-Americans, 5, 9, 11, 13, 21, 26
all-stars, 20
army, 9, 11
awards, 17, 19
Baseball Hall of Fame, 21
basketball, 7
batting, 15, 19
birth, 6
Brooklyn Dodgers, 12, 17, 19, 20, 21
children, 16
civil rights, 22
college, 7, 8
color barrier, 5, 17
death, 25
Ebbets Field, 17
family, 6, 16
fielding, 19
fiftieth-anniversary celebration, 26, 27
football, 7, 8

high school, 6
illnesses, 25
Jackson, Reverend Jesse, Jr., 25
Kansas City Monarchs, 11
Los Angeles Bulldogs, 8
major leagues, 5, 13, 15, 26
marriage, 16
Montreal Royals, 15
National League, 18, 19, 20
racism, 9, 17, 18, 22
retirement, 21, 22
Rickey, Branch, 12, 13, 17, 18
Robinson, Rachel Isum, 16, 26
school letter, 7
track, 7
University of California, 7
U.S. postage stamp, 26
World Series, 20
World War II, 9

About the Author

Lucia Raatma received her bachelor's degree in English literature from the University of South Carolina and her master's degree in cinema studies from New York University. She has written a wide range of books for young people. When she is not researching or writing, she enjoys going to movies, playing tennis, and spending time with her husband, daughter, and golden retriever.

jB
ROBINSON   Raatma, Lucia.

            Jackie Robinson.

$19.93

DATE			

FEB 28 2001

SOUTH HUNTINGTON
PUBLIC LIBRARY
2 MELVILLE ROAD
HUNTINGTON STATION, N.Y. 11746

BAKER & TAYLOR